ELIZABETHAN MINIATURES

by
CARL WINTER
Assistant Keeper
Victoria & Albert Museum

The KING PENGUIN *Books*
PUBLISHED BY PENGUIN BOOKS LIMITED
LONDON *and* NEW YORK
1943

THE KING PENGUIN BOOKS

Editor: N. B. L. Pevsner
Technical Editor: R. B. Fishenden

ACKNOWLEDGMENTS

THE author and editor are greatly indebted to His Majesty the King and the Librarian at Windsor, Mr. O. F. Morshead, to the Duke of Buccleuch, and to Sir Eric Maclagan, Director of the Victoria & Albert Museum, for courteously giving them permission and facilities to reproduce the miniatures illustrated in colour. For permission to reproduce Hillyarde's autograph thanks are due to Mr. W. Westley Manning, the owner of the document. The Hillyarde signature on p. 10 from the back of a miniature is reproduced by permission of the late Earl of Leicester.

The portrait of Queen Elizabeth on the cover is based upon part of a design by Hillyarde for a Great Seal of Ireland (Print Room, British Museum).

MADE IN GREAT BRITAIN

Text Pages printed by · *Colour Plates*
R. & R. CLARK, LTD., EDINBURGH · Colour blocks by W. F. SEDGWICK LTD.
Set in Monotype Baskerville · Printed by GEO. PULMAN & SONS LTD.

Cover design by
WILLIAM GRIMMOND

PUBLISHED BY

PENGUIN BOOKS LIMITED · PENGUIN BOOKS INC.
HARMONDSWORTH MIDDLESEX · 300 FOURTH AVENUE
ENGLAND · NEW YORK

In 1564 Sir James Melville, the emissary of Mary, Queen of Scots, had an interview with Queen Elizabeth. 'She took me', he relates in his *Memoirs*, 'to her bed-chamber, and opened a little cabinet, wherein were divers little pictures wrapped within paper, and their names written with her own hand upon the papers. Upon the first that she took up was written, *My Lord's picture*. I held the candle, and pressed to see the picture so named. She seemed loath to let me see it; yet my importunity prevailed for a sight thereof, and found it to be the *Earl of Leicester's* picture. I desired that I might have it to carry home to my Queen; which she refused, alleging that she had but that one picture of his. I said, your Majesty hath here the original; for I perceived him at the farthest part of the chamber, speaking with Secretary Cecil.'

The Earl of Rutland's accounts for 1586 included £80 'for a brooch of her Majestie's picture in an aggatt, set with 53 diamondes'. And when his nephew returned, in 1603, from an embassy to the King of Denmark, he and his suite were received by King James with marks of favour thus described in one of Philip Gawdy's letters: 'My Lo. of Rutland cam to courte last weeke, and some knightes and other gentlemen of the Kings servauntes to the number of sixtene had cheynes given them by the King with his picture hanging by the valewe of some thyrty or forty pounde. All the rest had his picture only.' An episode that chimes with Hamlet's words: 'My uncle is King of Denmark and those that would make mows at him while my father lived, give twenty, forty, fifty, a hundred ducats a-piece for his picture in little'.

3

These little pictures, which the Elizabethans also called 'limnings' and often wore in jewelled and enamelled lockets, are the portraits known to us as miniatures, a name which rightly describes the technique in which they were painted rather than their usually small size. In *A Treatise concerning the Arte of Limning*, composed about 1600 by Nicholas Hillyarde, who was limner to both Queen Elizabeth and to King James, the character and scope of the art are defined in terms which need no elaboration. Limning, said Hillyarde, is 'a thing apart from all other painting or drawing, and tendeth not to comon mens vsse, either for furnishing of howsses or any patternes for tapistries, or building, or any other work whatsoeuer, and yet it excelleth all other painting whatsoeuer in sondry points, in giuing the true lustur to pearle and precious stone, and worketh the metals gold or siluer with themselfes . . . benning fittest for the decking of princes bookes or to put in jeuuells of gould and for the imitation of the purest flowers and most beautifull creaturs in the finest and purest coullers . . . and is for the seruice of noble persons very meet in small voloms in priuat maner for theem to haue the portraits and pictures of themselues, their peers or any other. . . .'

The limner worked with fine brushes, then called 'pencils', largely in opaque water-colours, upon small sheets of special parchment stuck upon card, generally pieces of playing cards, cut into rounds, ovals or rectangles. His art and its technical processes derived from the practice of rubricating and illuminating manuscript-books with calligraphic decoration and pictures, as the word 'limning' is itself derived from 'illuminating'. The art of manuscript-illumination was moribund by the latter half of the sixteenth century, though one of the most celebrated of the later Flemish masters, Simon Benninck, survived to paint a self-portrait in the old style in 1558 (Pl. I b), the year when Queen Elizabeth ascended the English throne. Benninck does not appear to have worked in England, but there is no doubt that his style was familiar to the foreign limners employed by

Henry VIII. Benninck's daughter, Mrs. Livina Teer-linc, had migrated to England and appears to have doubled the rather incongruous rôles of miniaturist and nurse in the households of King Henry and his three children who succeeded him. Her career as an artist is a mystery, a matter of a few entries in official documents and a couple of references in contemporary lists of artists. She remains little more than a name: 'Mrs. Levyna Terling, paintrix' in receipt of an annuity of £40 'with her appointment during pleasure as King's nurse by letters under the signet dated at the Manor of Oteland, 28 Nov., 38 Henry viii' (Cal. Patent Rolls, I Eliz., p. 41).

Of the other foreign illuminators employed in England in the earlier part of the century, when the native school had already died out, no more need be said than that one of them, a Fleming, Lucas Horenbout (d. 1544), is supposed to have given Hans Holbein some instruction in miniature-painting. It was during his last years, while he was resident in England (1531–1543), that Holbein occasionally applied his mighty genius to the painting of portrait-miniatures. He was, Hillyarde observed, 'the most excelent painter and limner . . . the greatest master truly in both thosse arts after the liffe that euer was, so cuning in both together, and the neatest; and thewithall a good inuentor, soe compleat for all three as I neuer heard of any better then hee. . . . Holbeans maner of limning I haue euer imitated and howld it for the best, by reason that of truth all the rare siences, especially the arts of caruing, painting, gouldsmiths, imbroderers, together with the most of all the liberall siences, came first vnto vs from the strangers, and gener-ally they are the best and most in number.' The per-fection of Holbein's miniatures, exemplified by his *Anne of Cleves* and *Mrs. Pemberton* (Pls. I a and II a), set the style upon which Hillyarde consciously modelled himself and the standard by which his work must be judged.

The fragmentary story of Elizabethan limning has to be pieced together round the career of Hillyarde, who was not only an Englishman but that most famous breed of Elizabethan, a man of Devon. He developed the style, upon the foundations laid by Holbein; and during a long and illustrious career, in the various forms and combinations of art to which he devoted himself, he produced a mass of excellent work and some enchanting individual masterpieces which gained for him in his own age, at home and abroad, a renown that few other English artists have enjoyed or better deserved. His reputation attracted many pupils, and his post as royal limner obliged him to use their services, and no doubt the services of others, to keep pace with the demands made upon him for the multiplication of the sort of pictures which, as we have seen by one typical instance, monarchs were accustomed to bestow so liberally. The names of very few of these pupils and assistants have survived, but their works, evidently based upon Hillyarde's patterns and conforming to the superficial aspect of his style, are by no means uncommon. This is particularly noticeable among the opulent but generally rather tedious portraits of Queen Elizabeth and King James. It applies to some extent to miniatures of private persons also, which occasionally have several replicas. And there are many miniatures by more or less independent artists who either had some instruction from Hillyarde or merely sought to ape his manner.

The greatest of Hillyarde's pupils was a French Huguenot, Isaac Ollivier, known in England as Oliver. He became eventually a more fashionable painter than his former teacher, more realistic, dexterous and sophisticated, but with less inventive originality and nothing like Hillyarde's peculiar grace, refinement and gentle sensibility. While Hillyarde's name may be imaginatively linked with the Elizabethan poets, his miniatures being the counterparts in painting of Sidney's sonnets and the Arcadian idylls of Edmund Spenser, Oliver's mature work is like fine, hard, ornate prose, modelled upon the best masters, full of brazen Latinisms and choice quotations, and capable of nicely-calculated poetical flights, though not ethereal by nature. Both masters are delightful, each

6

in his way excellent, but it is hardly possible to appreciate them equally at any one moment.

Other pupils were Rowland Lockey (worked about 1590–1610), none of whose work can be identified, and Lawrence Hillyarde (1581/2–after 1640), Nicholas' only known son, who succeeded to his employment under King James, and produced competent but rather tame miniatures that develop little from his father's later official manner. Earlier artists who were active while Nicholas Hillyarde was growing from childhood to maturity, were John Shute (worked 1550–1570?), and the brothers, John (*d.* 1580?) and Thomas Bettes. No sequence of their work can be disentangled from the quantity of portraits that inherit something of the manner of Holbein. To these may be added the names, for instance, of Richard Haydocke and Henry Peacham, who were, and wished it to be clear that they were, gentlemen amateurs dabbling in the theory and practice of painting, perhaps including limning, about 1600 and after; and the herald, Edward Norgate (1581–1650), who painted miniatures (*e.g.* the portrait, rather in the style of Isaac Oliver, of his wife Judith, 1617, Pl. XVI b). Isaac Oliver's son, Peter (1594?–1647), was also an excellent limner, whose work far surpasses Lawrence Hillyarde's, but also lies principally within the next period, though examples are included here (Pl. XVI a and c) to show them both as legatees of their fathers' training. A few other artists are recorded, like A. van Brounckhurst and C. Devosse, who must be mentioned again presently, and there were still others whose names have vanished. But the tale of the company who worked with and about Hillyarde and Oliver in the period between 1560, when Hillyarde's active career began, and 1619, when he died, is now told in so far as it is known.

Very few indeed of Hillyarde's miniatures are signed and dated. Among these are two or three jejune works done when he was thirteen; a self-portrait in 1577 when he was thirty (Pl. III a); a portrait of his wife, Alice, in 1578 (Pl. III c); and a little portrait of a young man,

7

signed in full and dated 1599 at the back (signature and date are illustrated on p. 21). These documented works cover a period of forty years, 1560–1599. No signed and dated work is known to occur in the last two decades of Hillyarde's life, 1600–1619. There is in addition a fair number of unsigned miniatures, many of them dated, such as the 1577 portrait of Richard Hillyarde, the artist's father (Pl. III b); the portrait of Queen Elizabeth (Pl. IV a), in a gold and enamelled locket that is one of the most princely of English Renaissance jewels; the full-length of George Clifford, Earl of Cumberland, in the fanciful trappings of Queen's Champion (Pl. V); and the full length of a woebegone dandy, a lay figure of St. Sebastian, martyr to a lover's faithfulness, snared among roses and propping himself against a tree (Pl. VII), the embodiment of the spirit of Elizabethan love poetry and by general consent one of the prime masterpieces of English painting ; these and some dozens of other miniatures, though unsigned, can be securely attributed to Hillyarde, traditionally their author, with the characteristics of whose known style they faithfully agree.

Signed and dated miniatures by Isaac Oliver are less rare, though few in relation to his total output. But they cover the period 1583–1616, virtually the whole of his active career. Among them are a portrait of a man aged fifty-nine in 1588 (Collection of Her Majesty the Queen of Holland); Sir Arundell Talbot, 1596 (Pl. XI b), painted at Venice and inscribed at the back by the artist; a full-length portrait of the three Brothers Browne and a servant, 1598 (Burghley House); and a full-length portrait of Richard Sackville, third Earl of Dorset, 1616 (Pl. XV). Signed but undated Olivers are fortunately quite numerous and include some of his most remarkable miniatures; for example, the full-length portrait said to represent Sir Philip Sidney (Pl. VIII) and the profile of King James I's Queen, Anne of Denmark, wearing a costume for a masque (Pl. XIV b), both of which are at Windsor Castle; the profile of Henry Frederick, Prince of Wales, in 'Roman' costume (Pl. XIV a); a portrait of a

8

lady also wearing a masque costume (Pl. XIII b); and two splendid large circular miniatures, one said to represent the Countess of Bedford (Fitzwilliam Museum) and the other the Countess of Essex (Knowsley Hall).

Confrontation of these respective sets of miniatures by Hillyarde and Oliver shows at once the unmistakable difference between their aims and methods, and leaves small room for confusing their works. Because they were the two foremost artists of their time and calling, because they stood for a few years in the relation of master and pupil, and naturally employed similar technical materials, it has often been too easily forgotten that Hillyarde was a thorough Englishman, however far his curiosity caused him, as man and artist, to wander abroad; and that he was, in spite of his 'imitation' of Holbein, the inventor and exponent of a unique personal style. But Oliver was a Huguenot refugee in England, born in north-western France at a time when the arts of that region were deeply penetrated by influences from Flanders, whose painters were in turn themselves the willing slaves of their admiration for the Italian masters. He had inherited foreign sympathies from a father who was a Rouen goldsmith. Oliver lived, married, reared children and died in the bosom of the French, Flemish and Dutch refugee confraternity in London; and in 1596, during his trip to Venice, he described himself, like the uprooted Frenchman of Italian sympathies that he was, as 'Isacq oliuiero Francese' upon the back of a miniature (Pl. XI b), that is in character and lineaments a small brother of larger portraits by contemporary Flemings; and, whatever his reasons may have been or the change signified, he did not adopt English nationality until 1606, some eleven years before his death.

It would be fatuous to attempt to belittle Oliver's brilliant and various achievements upon the ground that he was less English than Hillyarde, and absurd to decry the work of one in order to praise the other. But it is a fact, though it is seldom recognised, that they were as different as English chalk and foreign cheese. There is

9

only a handful of miniatures dated between 1580–1582, when Oliver was apparently just emerging from Hillyarde's studio, which partake so equally of the manner of both painters that it is impossible to say which painted them. Thereafter their ways begin to part and they are hardly within hailing distance of one another by the end of their careers.

Nicholas, the eldest of the seven children of Richard Hillyarde, goldsmith, and his wife Laurence, daughter of John Wall, goldsmith, of London, was born at Exeter in or about 1547. The date is established by the inscription upon his self-portrait (Pl. III a) and his autograph: *Nicholas Hillyarde of London Goldsmithe at his age of iii^{xx}xi* (*i.e.* three score and eleven) *1617* (reproduced below), upon the back of a document that came to light only in 1933.

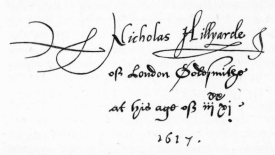

His brother, Jeremy, also became a goldsmith, and it may be observed that Nicholas in turn brought up his son, Lawrence, to be both goldsmith and limner; that Oliver was the son of a goldsmith; and that of the two men whose example exercised the greatest power over the formation of Hillyarde's style, Holbein made designs for goldsmiths' work that were even more decisive in their sphere of influence than his portrait-drawings and paintings in theirs, while Albrecht Dürer was the son of a goldsmith settled in Nuremberg. There is firsthand evidence in Hillyarde's letters and in State Papers that he was actively engaged in the goldsmith's craft all through his career. That he made medals and one of the Great Seals of England is known for certain; that his work included the making of lockets in which miniatures were often encased (such a locket is seen in Pl. XIV c) is very probable. It is, besides, likely that he practised engraving; and he may have painted some large pictures in oil, though one might well hesitate to pin any faith to the attribution of most of the oil paintings that have been fathered on him. The character of his miniature-paintings can only be rightly appreciated if they are seen as part, the central part, of this total activity, for they combine the arts of the jeweller, goldsmith and medallist as accessories to the art of the painter. That he chose to call himself a goldsmith is presumably due to there having been no guild or Company to which he could belong in any of his other capacities.

Hillyarde's father took an eminent part in the civic life of Exeter, becoming Bailiff and eventually Sheriff of the city. His name occurs upon the side of the Protestant loyalists when Exeter was besieged by the Cornish Catholic peasants during the Prayer-Book Rebellion in 1549. If, by 1558, young Nicholas had not already gone to London to be apprenticed, as has been supposed, to his grandfather, John Wall, he may have witnessed as an eleven-year-old the ghastly burning of heretics that took place in Exeter in the last days of Mary Tudor's reign.

When he was no more than eighteen, Nicholas is said to have painted a miniature of Mary, Queen of Scots, whose son, born in 1566, was later, as King of England, to become his patron and supporter during the last sixteen years of his career. It may perhaps have been a Hillyarde miniature of Mary that the watchful Spanish Ambassador reported, in 1566, having seen Queen Elizabeth ostentatiously wearing on a long gold chain from her waist. The date 1572 appears on a number of strikingly beautiful miniatures, including a famous portrait of Queen Elizabeth at the age of thirty-eight (National Portrait Gallery, No. 108) and the *Man aged 24* (Pl. II b), which typifies the quality of the whole of the group. The *Queen Elizabeth* is a singularly important genuine dated portrait of the Queen. It is drawn with all the delicate clarity of line, and the details are arranged with the felicity and painted with the loving skill that characterise Hillyarde's signed work of five years later. It is in every way likely that tradition is right in assigning it to his hand. These qualities also mark the portrait of the *Man aged 24* and the rest, and it is most probable that they are all by Hillyarde. But the need for caution in making such attributions may be emphasised by the tale of an event in which Hillyarde was involved about that year, 1572. He and two Flemish artists of his acquaintance, infected by the gold-fever that the Elizabethans could never get out of their systems, indulged in some speculative prospecting for gold in Scotland. There is no evidence that Hillyarde himself went to Scotland, but his servant and friend, Arnold or Arthur van Brounckhurst, made the trip, found a quantity of gold, was refused permission to remove it from the kingdom and was obliged to become 'one of his Majesties sworne servants at ordinary in Scotland, to draw all the small and great pictures for his Majesty'. His Majesty was King James VI, aged six. In 1580 van Brounckhurst was still holding his appointment as King's Limner in Scotland. The third partner in the venture was Cornelius Devosse, 'a most cuninge pictur maker', and if he was a limner too all that remains to be said is that every miniature by Hillyarde's two associates must have been misappropriated to other names, for none has survived in theirs.

It was four years before these events, in 1568, that Isaac Oliver arrived in London as a child accompanying his Huguenot parents. They were refugees from religious persecution in Rouen. In 1571 a return of aliens living in the Old Bailey quarter mentions 'Peter Oliver, sojourner within Harrisons howse, pewterer in Fletlane, goldsmythe, borne at Rone in Fraunce, and Typhan his wife, came into England iij yeres and dwelt in this parishe so longe, and hath one chyld named Isake, and as yeat no denizen'. They were only three of a total of nearly 5000 foreigners residing in London alone, a city estimated to have had about that time a population of some 93,000 souls. Many of the Dutch and Flemish immigrants were refugees from Alva's savageries in the Spanish Netherlands; the French were only an instalment of the numbers who, before and after the Massacre on St. Bartholomew's Day, 1572, came to seek, in the realm of the Queen of England, the safety which it then offered to Protestants of approved varieties. These 'strangers' included a host of artists and craftsmen of all kinds. Their English counterparts bore with what patience they might the advent of so many foreign competitors, ingenious, industrious, willing to work harder for smaller rewards, and authority had to exert itself to see both that 'murmuring against strangers' did not often issue in violence and that the strangers conformed to the laws of the land. But the importance of the foreign influence so brought to bear upon English life, the continuous effect upon thought, manners, fashion, and perhaps most obviously upon the arts, was immense and not susceptible of control. Henry Peacham's lament (*Graphice*, 1606), that 'our courtiers and great personages must seeke farre and neere for some dutchman or Italian to draw their pictures, and inuent their deuises, our Englishmen being held for *Vaunients* (good-for-nothings)', does not exaggerate the partiality of his contemporaries for foreign portrait-painters. It applies with less force to the limners, for Hillyarde's name was held in high esteem even when his style had passed the zenith of its favour and his pockets were empty, and Oliver's long residence allowed him to be regarded as a sort of Englishman before he became legally a 'denizen'. Nevertheless the foreign complexion of much of Oliver's work, most noticeable in his frankly Italianate drawings of biblical and classical subjects, though also clearly seen in many of his limned portraits, shows the colour that the work of the strangers and the snobbery of patrons combined to give to the arts in England.

But while Oliver was still a child, Hillyarde was already, in 1572, an established master of his art, painting from now on a succession of little pictures whose Maytime freshness and delicacy captivated the Queen and her courtiers and held their favour during thirty of the most tense and brilliant years in English history. By about 1576 Hillyarde was sufficiently well-established to be able to unite himself in marriage with Alice, the beautiful daughter of John Brandon, Chamberlain of the City of London. Their portraits show that they were a fair match in good looks, and suggest, like the portrait of Nicholas' father, Richard (all Pl. III), that they enjoyed a prosperous station in life. The Latin text Hillyarde added in the margin of the portrait of Alice is probably later than the portrait itself. It describes her as his first wife, but she seems to have lived at least long enough to mother his son, Lawrence, who was baptized at St. Vedast's, Foster Lane, 5th March 1581/2. Neither the date of her death nor of Nicholas' remarriage is known. His second wife presumably died before him, for she is not mentioned in his will.

Apart from their biographical interest these portraits, two of them signed and all dated, are exceptionally important illustrations of Hillyarde's limning technique. The portrait of his wife, one of the loveliest miniatures he ever painted, is somewhat damaged: the 'carnations' or flesh-tints have partly faded and partly been smudged onto the ruff. Worse things have happened to many others of his miniatures. Damp, heat, dirt, exposure to strong natural light and the hand of the restorer have reduced many of them to scarcely recognisable ghosts. It can only be upon the evidence of such unreliable witnesses that charges of 'flatness' and timidity have sometimes been levelled against Hillyarde's technique. For, while he rigorously eschewed all emphatic shadow effects and relied for modelling entirely upon gradual intensifications of pure colour, miniatures like the portraits of himself and his father, where the carnations still partly survive, or like the *Man aged 24*, where they are virtually intact, show that he was fully aware of the uses of modelling and practised it with extreme subtlety. His method is best described in his own words: 'Shadowing in lymning must not be driuen with the flat of the pensel (brush) as in oyle worke, distemper, or washing, but with the pointe of the pencell by littel light touches with cullor very thine, and like hatches as wee call it with the pen; though the shadowe be neuer so great it must be all so done by littel touches, and touch not to longe in one place, least it glisten, but let it dry ane howre or to, then dipen it again. Wherfore hatching with the pene, in imitation of some fine well grauen portrature of Albertus Dure (Dürer's) small peeces, is first to be practised and vsed, before one begine to limme, and not to learne to limme at all till one canne imitate the print so well as one shall not knowe the one frome the other, that he may be able to handle the pensill point in like sort. This is the true order and principall secret in limning, which that it maye be the better remembred, I end with it.'

Shadowing indicates mass, gives the subject depth and relief, effects that Hillyarde considered easily exaggerated in limning, which was not meant to tell from afar but to be held in the hand and closely examined. The limner should therefore rely chiefly upon line. This is his main thesis and he constantly recurs to it. He loses no opportunity of belabouring limners who 'smut' their pictures with shadows, which, he remarks, can only be useful when either artist or sitter has some blemish to conceal in such murk. The other remarkable feature of the passage quoted is the advice to beginners to get their hands in by slavish imitation of the prints of the great Nuremberg engraver and painter whom Hillyarde calls in another place 'the most excelent Albert Dure' and of whom he says: 'Dowbtles he was the most exquisite man that euer leaft vs lines to vieue for true delination, the most perfect shadower that euer graued in metal for true shadowes, and one of the best and truest in his perspectiue'. Hillyarde's references leave no doubt of his esteem for Dürer and the close attention that he had paid to Dürer's work. There are slight but discernible traces in his miniature of his father, of his study of Dürer's engraved portraits, no

of other properties to an annual value of over £40 in 1587. By 1591 he had become so adept at portraying the Queen that he could make a perfect likeness, as Sir John Harington noted, in four lines only; to which Hillyarde somewhat sharply adds 'as he might as well haue sayd in one lyne, but best in plaine lines without shadowing, for the lyne without shadowe showeth all to a good jugment, but the shadowe without lyne showeth nothing'. Exquisitely delineated and decorative as his original portraits of Elizabeth are, none of them approaches or aims at the candour and realism of Oliver's limning of her in her latter years (Pl. XII, with a portrait of her last favourite, the Earl of Essex). It was perhaps owing to Oliver's particularity in tracing the handiwork of time that the miniature remained unfinished. For the Queen showed a constantly diminishing enthusiasm for the play of tell-tale light and shade where her own ageing features were the subject.

By the end of the century, when the reign too was drawing towards its close, Oliver had become a formidable competitor to Hillyarde. It was all very well to be the royal limner, but it was no easy matter to wheedle one's pay from a notoriously stingy mistress. It was all very well to read in Richard Haydocke's inflated prose (*A Tracte Containinge The Artes of curious Paintinge*, etc., 1598) that 'M. Nicholas Hilliards hand, so much admired amongst strangers', might 'striue for a comparison with the milde spirit of the late worldes-wonder Raphaell Vrbine', but the hard facts were that Hillyarde was 'brought into great extremes' in 1599; and, as he wrote to Sir Robert Cecil in 1601, that he had 'taught divers, both strangers and English, which now and of a long time have pleased the common sort exceeding well, so that I am myself unable by my art any longer to keep house in London without some farther help of her Majesty'. The *Treatise*, composed about this time, is full of laments upon the hard lot of a painter not worthily employed and rewarded, like a precious stone ill-set and sold for naught. 'Whoe doubts of that?' cries Hillyarde. 'It is the like of me.' And when he recounts the miseries of another artist, 'only unfortunat becasse he was English borne, for euen the strangers would otherwisse haue set him vpp', the point of the reference is perfectly plain.

It may be surmised that fashionable persons did not sufficiently hearken to his admonition that 'noe wisse man longer remaine in error of praysing much shadowes in pictures after the life, especially small pictures which ar to be wiued in hand . . .'; nor care for his outmoded opinion that 'a picture a littel shadowed may be bourne withall for the rounding of it, but so greatly smutted or darkned as some vsse disgrace it, and is like truth ill towld'. Miniatures with such dramatic chiaroscuro (Pls. IX a; XV) are not uncommon among Isaac Oliver's works, and though the effect is more suitable to large-scale oil painting, from which it was borrowed, it was finding increasing favour. Peter Oliver afterwards carried the practice sometimes to extreme limits (Pl. XVI c).

Queen Elizabeth died in 1603. Hillyarde survived her by sixteen years. During that period he painted some magnificent miniatures which show no trace whatever of declining powers, in spite of the decline of health of which he complained. King James had immediately confirmed him in his official post and he seems to have earned at least his bread and butter thenceforth chiefly by painting, or rather manufacturing, miniatures of his new royal patron, and by making the King's gold medals, tasks in which his son Lawrence aided him, and to which he eventually succeeded. The King seems to have paid Hillyarde regularly and he also enjoyed the protection of Cecil, from 1605 Earl of Salisbury and Secretary of State until his death in 1612. In 1617 the King issued a most comprehensive licence granting Hillyarde 'in respect of his extraordinary Art and Skill in Drawing, Graving and Imprinting of Pictures and Representations of Vs and others' the exclusive right for twelve years 'to Invent, Make, Grave and Ymprint any Picture or Pictures of our Image, or other Representation of our Person'. In the same year, upon the back of the anagram, *En Christ ay la loi*, sent him by Jehan Durant, Hillyarde wrote his name in his beautifully clear firm hand. Next year, in London, on Christmas Eve, 'sick in body but of perfect mynde & memory', he made his will and could sign it with no more than a mark feebly caricaturing the monograms he had written upon the portraits of himself and his wife over forty years before. The will hastily and briefly disposes of the household furniture and the hypothetical estate of one who was clearly not rich. On the 7th January 1619 he was buried in the yard of his parish church, St. Martin-in-the-Fields. Of him we may take leave in the words with which he ended one of his letters to Cecil: 'even Moyses had his ffault in speche, but his hart was wth God (most ffaythfull) To whome I comitt yor Hono^r. . . .'

Oliver had predeceased Hillyarde by fifteen months. He was buried on 2nd October 1617 in St. Anne's, Blackfriars, a church destroyed in the Great Fire and not rebuilt. His will is a long and formidably premeditated legal document, settling with proper safeguards an estate that was evidently the carefully-tended fruit of an industrious, prudent and successful career. He was, says the translator of De Piles's *Art of Painting*, 1706, 'eminent both for History and Faces . . . a very good designer, his Drawings were finished to a mighty Perfection, some of them being admirable copies after *Parmeggiano*, &c. . . . He was very neat and curious in his Limnings. . . . He was likewise a very good Oil-Painter in *Little*.' His work found great favour with James I's Queen, Anne of Denmark, with their brilliant, short-lived son, Henry Frederick, Prince of Wales (Pl. XIV a and b), with their daughter, Elizabeth, the 'Winter Queen', and her husband Frederick of Bohemia, and King James's cousin, Lady Arabella Stuart. Miniatures such as his profiles of Prince Henry, in 'Roman' costume, like a cameo or a tinted classical bust in its Palladian niche; the profile of Anne of Denmark and the portrait of a lady (Pl. XIII b), both in costumes worn, it is supposed, in the magnificent Court Masques written by Ben Jonson and designed by the great architect, Inigo Jones; such a lavishly splendid work as the full-length portrait of Richard Sackville, Earl of Dorset (Pl. XV), like a small-scale version of an oil-painting by Oliver's brother-in-law, Marcus Gheeraerts the Younger (1561–1635), sufficiently explain how Oliver managed to bear the palm away from Hillyarde in the last years of their lives, and why since then many have continued to hold his work in equal or higher esteem. His adaptable spirit was more easily attuned to the classicizing taste of the new age. He was also a straightforward portrait-painter in a way that Hillyarde, with his linear convention of drawing, his jeweller's dream of capturing in paint the colours of diamond, sapphire, ruby, emerald, topaz and amethyst, his goldsmith's passion for decoration, his medallist's concentration upon pattern and low relief, never had been, and never sought to become. But to the invidious question, which of the two—both equally 'little masters' in comparison with Holbein—was the finer limner and the truer Elizabethan, some may still be found to reply in the well-known lines of John Donne:

> a hand, or eye
> By *Hilliard* drawne, is worthy an history
> By a worse painter made.
> (*The Storme*, 1597)

LIST OF PLATES

Note: The miniatures are in water-colour on parchment, mostly stuck on playing-card or other card. Inscriptions in gold.

I. HANS HOLBEIN THE YOUNGER (1497?–1543).

(a) THE PRINCESS ANNE OF CLEVES (1515–1557).

Round. Diameter $1\frac{23}{32}$ in.

Victoria & Albert Museum (P. 153-1910; Salting Bequest). Painted about 1539 with the half-length portrait now belonging to the Musée du Louvre, Paris (No. 2718). Anne, fourth wife of King Henry VIII (1491–1547), married 6th January, divorced 12th July 1540. The miniature is in a turned ivory box of rose form.

(See: A. B. Chamberlain, *H.H. the Younger*, 1913, vol. II, pp. 181-182.)

SIMON BENNINCK (1483/4–1561).

(b) SELF-PORTRAIT AT THE AGE OF 75 (1558).

Inscribed: ·SIMÕ·BINNIK·ALEXÃDRI·F^8
                SEIPSṼ·PĨGEBAT·ANO·ÆTATIS 75
                                1558

Rectangular: $3\frac{7}{32} \times 2\frac{3}{32}$ in.

Victoria & Albert Museum (P. 159-1910; Salting Bequest). See p. 4.

(See: W. H. J. Weale, *Burlington Magazine*, vol. VIII, 1906, pp. 355-357; and F. Winkler, *Die Flämische Buchmalerei*, etc., Leipzig, 1925, pp. 139-149.)

II. HANS HOLBEIN THE YOUNGER (1497?–1543).

(a) MRS. PEMBERTON (*d.* 1576).

Inscribed: ·ANNO·ETATIS·SVÆ·23·

Round. Diameter $2\frac{1}{16}$ in.

Victoria & Albert Museum (P. 40-1935; Funds of Captain H. B. Murray's Bequest with donations from Viscount Bearsted and the National Art-Collections Fund). Believed to represent Margaret Throckmorton, wife of Robert Pemberton (*d.* 1594). The miniature appears to date from about 1540–1543. Formerly in the Pierpont Morgan Collection (Sale, Christie's 24.6.1935, Lot 125, bought for £6195 by the late Lord Duveen, who ceded it to the Museum at the same price).

(See: A. B. Chamberlain, *loc. cit.* pp. 228-229; V. & A. M., *Annual Review*, 1935, pp. 28-29.)

NICHOLAS HILLYARDE (about 1547–1619).

(b) MAN AGED 24, 1572.

Inscribed: Ætatis Sue·xxiiii·Anõ·Dm̃·1572.

Rectangular: 2⅜ × 1⅞ in.

Victoria & Albert Museum (P. 1-1942). The identity of the
subject, evidently a young nobleman, is unknown. The
technique resembles that of Hillyarde's signed miniatures
of 1577 and 1578. Formerly in the Buccleuch Collection:
presented to the Museum by the National Art-Collections
Fund, 1942.

III. NICHOLAS HILLYARDE (about 1547–1619).

(a) SELF-PORTRAIT, AGED 30, 1577.

Inscribed: Anõ Dm̃·1577 Ætatis Suæ 30. Signed with cursive
monogram: N.H.

Round. Diameter: 1¹⁹⁄₃₂ in.

Victoria & Albert Museum (P. 155-1910; Salting Bequest).
The miniature appears at one time to have had a border
with a Latin inscription describing Hillyarde as Gold-
smith, Sculptor (Engraver) and celebrated Limner to
Queen Elizabeth. In its medallic shape and design it is
akin to Germin Pilon's medals of Charles IX (1573) and
Henri III (1575), Kings of France. (See: J. Babelon,
Germain Pilon, Paris, 1927, plates LII and LIII.)

(b) RICHARD HILLYARDE (1518/19–1594), AGED 58, 1577, FATHER
OF THE ARTIST.

Inscribed: Ætatis Suæ 58: Anno Dm̃ 1577.

Round. Diameter: 1²¹⁄₃₂ in.

Victoria & Albert Museum (P. 154-1910; Salting Bequest).
The miniature is a companion-piece to the self-portrait
above, and has the same history. It also appears to have
once had a border with a Latin inscription.

(c) ALICE BRANDON, AGED 22, 1578, HILLYARDE'S FIRST WIFE.

Inscribed: Anõ Dm̃·1578·Æs S·22·. Signed twice with monogram: NH. Border inscribed: ALICIA·BRANDON·NICOLAI
HILLYARDI·QVI PROPRIA MANV DEPINXIT VXOR PRIMA:·

Oval mounted in a round. Diameter: 2⁵⁄₁₆ in.

Victoria & Albert Museum (P. 2-1942). See p. 14. Shields of
arms of Brandon (right) and of Hillyarde. One of Hillyarde's few signed and dated works. Formerly in the
Buccleuch Collection: presented to the Museum by the
National Art-Collections Fund, 1942.

23

IV. NICHOLAS HILLYARDE (about 1547–1619).

(a) QUEEN ELIZABETH (1533–1603).

Oval. $2\frac{13}{32} \times 1\frac{27}{32}$ in.

Victoria & Albert Museum (4404-1857). 'Next came the queen, very majestic, her face oblong, fair, but wrinkled, her eyes small, yet black and pleasant; her nose a little hooked, her lips thin, and her teeth black. She had in her ears two pearls, with very rich drops; she wore false hair, and that red; upon her head she had a small crown. Her bosom was uncovered, as all the English ladies have it till they marry; and she had on a necklace of exceeding fine jewels . . .' (Paul Hentzner's *Itinerary*, 1598, trans. Horace Walpole). The case of this miniature is of gold decorated at the back with a design of dolphins and foliage in white, red, green, blue and yellow *champlevé* enamel upon a black ground; the lid is of pierced gold, enamelled and set with rubies and diamonds in a sunray and scroll-ing pattern. (See: Joan Evans, *English Jewellery*, London, Methuen, 1921, p. 101, p. xx.)

(b) MAN CLASPING A HAND FROM A CLOUD.

Inscribed: Attici amoris ergo. Anô·Dm̃·1588·

Oval. $2\frac{3}{8} \times 1\frac{31}{32}$ in.

Victoria & Albert Museum. Painted in the year of the defeat of the Great Armada. The identity of the subject and the meaning of the motto are unknown. A similar miniature, wrongly described as a portrait of the Earl of Essex and attributed to Isaac Oliver, was formerly at Castle Howard. Transferred from the British Museum (Sloane No. 272). Damaged.

V. NICHOLAS HILLYARDE (about 1547–1619).

GEORGE CLIFFORD, 3RD EARL OF CUMBERLAND, K.G. (1558–1605), QUEEN'S CHAMPION.

Rectangular. 10⅛ × 7 in.

From the Collection of His Grace the Duke of Buccleuch. One of the largest, most celebrated and picturesque of Hillyarde's works, this miniature nevertheless shows his art stretched somewhat beyond its effective power. It depicts a colourful Elizabethan sailor in the fancy costume of Queen's Champion. Apparently painted before Cumberland was created a K.G. (1592), and may commemorate the tilting on 17th November 1590, when he was first accepted as Champion. He wears the Queen's glove pinned to his hat and his shield is decorated with a riddling *impresa,* or device, of the earth between sun and moon, with a Spanish motto, *Hasta quan* . . . The distant landscape is adapted from the stock scenery used by Dürer in the background of a number of his engravings and woodcuts.

VI. NICHOLAS HILLYARDE (about 1547–1619).

(a) QUEEN ELIZABETH (1533–1603)

Oval. 2¹⁹⁄₃₂ × 2⅛ in.

Victoria & Albert Museum (622-1882; Jones Collection). Formerly in Horace Walpole's Collection at Strawberry Hill. 'A pale Roman nose, a head of hair loaded with crowns and powdered with diamonds, a vast ruff . . . and a bushel of pearls, are the features by which everybody knows at once the pictures of Queen Elizabeth', wrote Horace Walpole. The 'carnations' or flesh-tints and the crimson of the curtain in the background have completely faded. The silver high-lights on the pearls and the silver ornaments on the ruff have turned black. The miniature is therefore only a ghost of its original self, though it remains a magnificent costume-piece.

(See: V. & A.M., B. S. Long, *Catalogue of the Jones Collection,* Part III, 1923, pp. 80-81.)

(b) A MAN AGAINST A BACKGROUND OF FLAMES.

Oval. $2\frac{23}{32} \times 2\frac{1}{8}$ in.

Victoria & Albert Museum (P 5-1917; Funds of Captain H. B. Murray's Bequest). The image of the lover 'burning in flames beyond all measure' is frequent in Renaissance literature. Clad in his fine linen shirt and holding a locket, doubtless containing a portrait of his mistress, towards his heart, the lover is here evidently supposed to be suffering martyrdom at the stake. Previously attributed to Isaac Oliver, but both in conception and technique it is purely typical of Hillyarde's work. The card upon which the parchment is stuck is the ace of hearts. (See: V. & A.M., *Annual Review*, 1917, pp. 44-45.)

VII. NICHOLAS HILLYARDE (about 1547–1619).

A YOUTH LEANING AGAINST A TREE AMONG ROSES.

Inscribed: Dat pœnas laudata fides:

Oval. $5\frac{9}{32} \times 2\frac{13}{16}$ in.

Victoria & Albert Museum (P. 163-1910; Salting Bequest). The motto, which may be translated, 'My praisèd faith procures my pain', recalls many similar lines in the poems of the Elizabethan amorists (*e.g.* 'My tryed truth entangleth me in trayne', in a poem in *The Gorgious Gallery of Gallant Inuentions*, 1578). The victim of these unmerited sufferings is anonymous. He can be taken for any courtly Corydon with 'a pair of stockings white as milk' upon 'his legs so tall' (*Phyllida's Love-call*). Costume about 1590. There is a head-and-shoulders miniature by Hillyarde of the same youth, aged 22 in 1588, in the Metropolitan Museum, New York (Accession No. 35.89.4; formerly at Warwick Castle, later in the J. P. Morgan Collection).

VIII. ISAAC OLIVER (*d.* 1617).

PORTRAIT OF A YOUNG MAN, SAID TO BE SIR PHILIP SIDNEY (1554–1586).

Signed: IO (monogram).

Rectangular. $4\frac{5}{8} \times 3\frac{1}{4}$ in.

Collection of His Majesty The King, Windsor Castle. This famous miniature, one of Oliver's chief works, is usually regarded as a portrait of Sidney, but the youthfulness of the subject and the later style of the costume make this identification uncertain. The composition is based upon a reversal of Dürer's engraving, *The Madonna with the Pear* (Bartsch 41).

IX. ISAAC OLIVER (*d.* 1617).

(a) MAN AGED 27, 1590.
   Inscribed: Ano Dm̃ 1590·Ætatis Suæ 27·
   Oval. $2\frac{1}{16} \times 1\frac{3}{4}$ in.
   Victoria & Albert Museum (P. 37-1941; given by Mrs. Samuel
      S. Joseph). Dramatic light and shade is often found in
      Oliver's works; the realistic modelling of hand and ear is
      in strong contrast to the highly stylised hands and ears in
      portraits by Hillyarde.

(b) GIRL AGED 5, 1590, HOLDING A RED CARNATION.
   Inscribed in gold: Ano Dm̃·1590·Ætatis Suæ·5.
   Oval. $2\frac{1}{8} \times 1\frac{11}{16}$ in.
   Victoria & Albert Museum (P. 146-1910; Salting Bequest).
      Enclosed in the halves of an ivory case. Both these delight-
      ful miniatures, though not so heavily shadowed, are in
      every respect technically identical with the portrait of the
      Man aged 27, 1590, reproduced on this plate. It has been
      alleged that the little girls were painted at Greenwich by
      Livina Teerlinc (concerning whom, see p. 5). The date
      makes this unlikely, while they exactly correspond with
      Oliver's style.

(c) GIRL AGED 4, 1590, HOLDING AN APPLE.
   Inscribed: Ano Dm̃·1590·Ætatis Suæ·4.
   Oval. $2\frac{1}{8} \times 1\frac{11}{16}$ in.
   Victoria & Albert Museum (P. 145-1910; Salting Bequest).

X. NICHOLAS HILLYARDE (about 1547–1619).

(a) LADY WITH A FLEUR-DE-LYS JEWEL.
   Oval. $2\frac{7}{8} \times 2\frac{1}{8}$ in.
   Fitzwilliam Museum, Cambridge. Court costume of 1585–90.
      Identity unknown. Formerly in the Buccleuch Collection.

(b) A KNIGHT OF THE GARTER, 1605.
   Inscribed: Anδ Dm̃.1605.
   Oval. $1\frac{29}{32} \times 1\frac{19}{32}$ in.
   Collection of His Grace the Duke of Buccleuch. The flesh-tints
      have faded. Painted two years after the death of Queen
      Elizabeth. The latest miniature by Hillyarde here repro-
      duced, though splendid dated examples of his work occur
      as late as 1616. The identity of the subject is unknown.
   Both these miniatures are characteristic of Hillyarde's style
      and may be accepted as original works by him, though
      the *Lady with a fleur-de-lys jewel* has sometimes been taken
      for an Oliver.

XI. NICHOLAS HILLYARDE (about 1547–1619).

(a) 'MRS. HOLLAND', AGED 26, 1593.

Inscribed: Anõ Dnĩ·1593·Ætatis suæ·26.

Oval. $2\frac{9}{32} \times 1\frac{29}{32}$ in.

Victoria & Albert Museum (P. 134-1910; Salting Bequest).
Court costume. Said to represent Mrs. Holland, one of
Queen Elizabeth's Maids of Honour.

ISAAC OLIVER (*d.* 1617).

(b) 'SIR ARUNDELL TALBOT,' 1596.

Inscribed at back by the artist: adi. i̇3. Magio. 1596. In
Venetia. Fecit m. Isacq oliùiero Francese 10 (monogram) ṽ. i4. da L 8. And in another hand: Viva & vera
effigies Arundelli Talbot Equitis Aurati.

Oval. $2\frac{3}{4} \times 2\frac{3}{16}$ in., within an octangle.

Victoria & Albert Museum (P. 4-1917; Funds of Captain H. B.
Murray's Bequest). The flesh-tints have faded. The
signed inscription in Italian at the back shows that Oliver
was in Venice in 1596 and that he considered himself, as
he was both legally and spiritually, a Frenchman.
Venice, perhaps even more than Rome, was the magnet
that attracted Italianising Northern artists in the late
sixteenth century, and an international colony of expat-
riate Flemish, German and other painters, engravers, etc.,
was busily employed there translating into Northern
terms the art of Titian, Tintoretto and Veronese. The
miniature shows that Oliver's style was affected by the
portrait work of contemporary Flemish and Dutch artists.

XII. ISAAC OLIVER (*d.* 1617).

(a) QUEEN ELIZABETH (1533–1603).

Oval. $2\frac{7}{16} \times 2\frac{3}{32}$ in.

Victoria & Albert Museum (P. 8-1940; Funds of the R. H.
Stephenson Bequest). Compare with Hillyarde's por-
traits of the Queen (Pls. IV a and VI a). See p. 18.
Bought at the H. Reynolds Solly Sale at Sotheby's, 27th
June 1940; may once have belonged to Dr. Richard Mead
(1673–1754).

(See: F. M. O'Donoghue, *Portraits of Queen Elizabeth*,
London, 1894, p. 32, No. 29, and p. 34.)

(b) ROBERT DEVEREUX, 2ND EARL OF ESSEX, K.G. (1566–1601).
Oval. $2 \times 1\frac{5}{8}$ in.
Collection of His Majesty The King, Windsor Castle. An authentic portrait of Queen Elizabeth's favourite, who was executed for high treason. He wears the ribbon of the Garter.

XIII. ISAAC OLIVER (*d.* 1617).

(a) A MAN, UNKNOWN.

Oval. $1\frac{15}{16} \times 1\frac{5}{8}$ in.
Collection of His Grace the Duke of Buccleuch. Characteristic of Oliver's style about 1610. The forehead restored. In a gold locket enamelled black.

(b) LADY IN MASQUE COSTUME.

Signed: IO (monogram).
Oval. $2\frac{1}{2} \times 2$ in.
Victoria & Albert Museum (P. 3-1942). One of Oliver's loveliest miniatures, with an unusual colour-scheme. The dress is in the style of Inigo Jones's superb designs for costumes worn in Ben Jonson's Masques performed at the Court of James I. Formerly in the Buccleuch Collection; presented to the Museum by the National Art-Collections Fund, 1942.

XIV. ISAAC OLIVER (*d.* 1617).

(a) HENRY FREDERICK, PRINCE OF WALES (1594–1612).

Signed: IO (monogram).
Oval. $2\frac{1}{16} \times 1\frac{5}{8}$ in.
Fitzwilliam Museum, Cambridge. Two profile portraits by Oliver in the Jacobean classical style. The Queen is wearing what seems to be a masque costume (see note to Pl. XIII b); and her elder son, who died aged 18, is seen in 'Roman' costume with a grey stone alcove in the background. Replicas of (a) are in the Royal Collection, Windsor Castle, and in the National Portrait Gallery.

(b) ANNE OF DENMARK (1574–1619), QUEEN OF JAMES I.

Signed: IO (monogram). Inscribed: Seruo per regnare.
Oval.
Collection of His Majesty The King, Windsor Castle.

ASCRIBED TO ISAAC OLIVER (*d.* 1617).

(c) A LADY, UNKNOWN, AGED 50.

Inscribed: Ætatis Suæ·50·
Oval. 2$\frac{3}{16}$ × 1$\frac{3}{4}$ in.
Victoria & Albert Museum (P. 24-1932; Funds of Captain H.
  B. Murray's Bequest). She wears a miniature locket (pig-
  ment flaked) similar to the gold locket, with an incised
  diaper pattern covered with claret-coloured transparent
  enamel, in which her own portrait is encased. Costume of
  about 1615. The miniature much resembles Isaac
  Oliver's style, and is probably by him. A suggested
  identification as a self-portrait of Levina Teerlinc (see:
  Burlington Magazine, vol. LXIV, 1934, p. 232 *et seq.*), is
  impossible upon score of date.
(See: V. & A.M., *Annual Review*, 1932, pp. 29–30.)

XV. ISAAC OLIVER (*d.* 1617).

RICHARD SACKVILLE, 3RD EARL OF DORSET (1589–1624).

Signed and dated: Isaac. Olliuierus. fecit. 1616.
Rectangular. 9$\frac{1}{4}$ × 6 in.
Victoria & Albert Museum (721-1882; Jones Collection). One
  of Oliver's largest and most imposing miniatures, reflect-
  ing the fashionable style of oil-paintings by Marcus
  Gheeraerts the Younger (1561–1635), Oliver's brother-
  in-law.
(See: V. & A.M., B. S. Long, *Catalogue of the Jones Collection*,
  Part III, 1923, p. 86.)

XVI. LAWRENCE HILLYARDE (1582–after 1640).

(a) LADY WEARING A WIDE-BRIMMED BLACK HAT.

Signed: LH· (monogram).
Oval. 2$\frac{3}{16}$ × 1$\frac{13}{16}$ in.
Victoria & Albert Museum. Costume of about 1615–30. Attributed by reason of the monogram, to Nicholas Hillyarde's
  son, his successor as Royal Limner. Transferred from
  the British Museum.

EDWARD NORGATE (1581–1650).

(b) JUDITH NORGATE, *née* LARNER, AGED 25, 1617, WIFE OF THE ARTIST.

Inscribed at back by the artist: Juditha Norgate. 1617·æt: 25. Non obijt sed abijt. Pudicitiæ, Pietatis, et Venustatis rarissimum decus. Suauissimæ Conjugi Ed: Norgate.

Oval. $2\frac{5}{32} \times 1\frac{23}{32}$ in.

Victoria & Albert Museum (P. 71-1935; Funds of Captain H. B. Murray's Bequest). Norgate was appointed Windsor Herald (1633) and Clerk of the Signet (1638); celebrated for his illuminated penmanship in Royal Patents, letters to foreign princes, etc.; wrote a valuable treatise called *Miniatura or the Art of Limning* (Clarendon Press, Oxford, 1919, ed. Martin Hardie, from the MS. preserved in the Bodleian Library). This miniature is attributed to Norgate upon the strength of the inscription, which may be translated '. . . She has not died: she has departed. Rarest ornament of Modesty, Affection and Beauty. To his most sweet wife, Ed: Norgate.' Norgate remarried in 1619.

(See: V. & A.M., *Annual Review*, 1935, p. 29.)

PETER OLIVER (1594?–1647).

(c) SIR FRANCIS NETHERSOLE (1587–1659).

Signed: PO (monogram). Inscribed: Anno Dõn.1619·32 En. Vous. Voyant:

Oval. $2 \times 1\frac{5}{8}$ in.

Victoria & Albert Museum (P. 6-1917; Funds of Captain H. B. Murray's Bequest). Sir F. Nethersole, sometime tutor at Trinity College, Cambridge, and Public Orator to the University; in 1619 appointed Secretary to Elizabeth, Queen of Bohemia, and knighted.

(See: V. & A.M., *Annual Review*, 1917, p. 44.)

BIBLIOGRAPHICAL NOTE

THE standard work of reference is B. S. LONG's *British Miniaturists, 1520–1860*, London, 1929, a monumental dictionary with copious references to the previous literature of the subject. In addition to works cited in the notes to the List of Plates, the following give valuable information: R. W. GOULDING, *The Welbeck Abbey Miniatures*, Oxford, Walpole Society, vol. IV, 1916; L. CUST, *Foreign Artists of the Reformed Religion working in London, 1560–1660*, London, Huguenot Society, VII, i, 1903, pp. 45–82; JOAN EVANS, *Huguenot Goldsmiths in England, etc., ibid.* XIV, iv, 1933; HELEN FARQUHAR, *N. Hilliard, 'Embosser of Medals of Gold'*, London, Numismatic Chronicle, 4th Series, no. 32, 1908, pp. 324–356. HILLYARDE's *Treatise concerning the Arte of Limning*, printed from the MS. in Edinburgh University Library, with an introduction and notes by P. NORMAN, Oxford, Walpole Society, vol. I, 1912, pp. 1–54, is a document of capital importance. C. H. COLLINS BAKER and W. G. CONSTABLE, *English Painting of the 16th & 17th Centuries*, Paris, 1930, deal with large-scale portraiture; and the Oxford University Press, *Shakespeare's England*, 2 vols., 1916, and J. E. NEALE, *Queen Elizabeth*, London, 1934, with social, political and other aspects of the Elizabethan Age.

(a) *Hans Holbein* 1539 *(?)*
(b) *Simon Benninck* 1558

(a) Hans Holbein
(b) Nicholas Hillyarde 1572

Nicholas Hillyarde (*a*) 1577 (*b*) 1577
(*c*) 1578

(a) Nicholas Hillyarde (b) Nicholas Hillyarde 1588

Nicholas Hillyarde 1590 *(?)*

Nicholas Hillyarde

Nicholas Hillyarde

VIII

(Copyright of H.M. The King)

Isaac Oliver

Isaac Oliver 1590

(a) Nicholas Hillyarde
(b) Nicholas Hillyarde 1605

(a) Nicholas Hillyarde 1593
(b) Isaac Oliver 1596

(Copyright of H.M. The King)

Isaac Oliver

Isaac Oliver

XIV

(Copyright of H.M. The King)

Isaac Oliver

Isaac Oliver 1616

XVI

(a) Lawrence Hillyarde (b) Edward Norgate 1617
(c) Peter Oliver